And Now I
$\mathcal{L}$ive

Nathalie Chase Thompson

AND NOW I LIVE: MY STORY, MY TRUTH
Volume 1

Published by MIGMIR Company USA, LLC
P.O. BOX 721688 Orlando, Florida 32872

www.migmir.us

For Worldwide Distribution
Printed in the U.S.A.

ISBN: 9780997347739

Library of Congress Catalog Number: 2018946830

CONTENTS

ACKNOWLEDGEMENTS

To my mother, Pauline C. Chase, you've forever been my number one cheerleader; for that I am eternally thankful. When I was growing up I put your through hell but you never gave up on me. Look at us now, you are the Mother in Zion of LifesReDesign Ministry Intl, Inc. Nobody but God could have done this.

To the late Elder Jessie Mae Lester, founder of ARISE Christian Center, you truly birthed me out as one of the midwives in the Spirit. The weekends that we would shut up in your apartment and pray, talk, fast, laugh and cry, have not been in vain. Your rebuke caused me to be able to stand the test of times. You brought me and my children as your own family. They still stand today as sisters and brothers because of how you raised them. I thank God for you, such a priceless jewel. Rest well until we meet again.

To Elder Essie Mae Jones (Mama Jones) from day one of walking into (what was at the time) All People Church of God in Christ, my life was never the same. Sitting directly behind you and next to Missionary Jessie Lester at that time, God set me up. You two were the first to show me how to be transparent and naked before God, and that has shaped my life for divine destiny.

Chief Apostle Arthur T. Jones, Sr. I never knew March 1976-- seeing and hearing you preach from a distance, that you would become my father. You are a father indeed. Words can't express my gratitude for you raising and covering me for these 27 years and even now from a distance. 1000-fold blessing be unto you even the more.

Bishop Sharon P. Jones (my pretty lady) as I refer to her in private. She is my "iron sharpens iron" in the spirit. For that reason, the healings were bearable as God took me through the process.

(Continued at the back of the book)

DEDICATIONS

This is dedicated to all who have lost their way;

have been hurt

have lost everything

have been abused

have been labeled.

To you that have had "word curses" spoken over your life for so long, you now believe them--therefore, you "act" the part.

Maybe you were abandoned and left for dead. (even in the church, or so others have said.)

Just as well, if you need a little encouragement. You may have already come through the valley and now are heading towards another mountain top experience.

We are NOT what "they" say we are, ONLY what and who GOD calls us!

In Memory of the Late Leo Curtis Chase Sr., my loving father, now my angel. Thank you for watching over me. Those days, weeks and months that I thought I wouldn't make it. I'd smell that pipe or see you leaning against the post on the back porch of the funeral home and smile. For all of your smiles, kisses and warm hugs, I will forever love you daddy, see you in paradise.

FOREWORD

Truth is the one thing that will make you free. Unfortunately the average person does not really want what they need. In this book, Dr. Thompson opens her heart and gives you an "all access" look into pain, challenge, frustration and personal setback. She walks you through the real truth on how it affects you, and better yet—the answer to overcome it. Not many people will share their heart because many see that as vulnerable. It takes a heart of Agape to unashamedly give information that can be applied to others' lives and redirect them toward their God given purpose and divine assignment.

Dr. Thompson uses biblical examples and spiritual illustrations to outline the success strategy that worked for her and that will work for you. Take the time to read this book and personally evaluate yourself so that you can see the power of this book and share its value with others that need to grow to the new level they desire. You will be better after reading it; not only for yourself, but also for others.

Grayson Marshall, Jr. "The Metacognition Expert"

President and CEO, DoPositiveSwag®/Professor Positive

INTRODUCTION

Let me begin with saying, for those of you that will read through this book in its entirety I pray it SHALL be nothing but a blessing to you. Now at times so many emotions may arise, but push forward. There will be times of laughter, tears, frustration, confusion and oh yeah disbelief, keep reading. The content can and will reach beyond gender, economical and educational statuses, political views, nationalities, religious beliefs etc. If you doubt this could be possible continue to read.

This is not a fictitious book. It is in fact my life that I have lived. Some names were changed for the purpose of discretion. "And Now I Live" is being released in hopes that people will be able to get FREE for real. Free from mental, emotional, religious, financial and self-inflicted bondages-- just to mention a few.

Through this journey I've been blessed. I am a Pastor, wife, mother and grandmother. With those successes I've also been a recipient of incest, rape, and homelessness to name a few. Now on the other hand, I've been quite bitter (you do know at times the abused becomes the abuser), BUT GOD! Now in my mid 50's, I've walked in ministry for over 24yrs and I understand and have accepted the life HE mapped out for me.

Through these pages you will hear much. Always remember, I never gave up on God. For the Jobs, Josephs, Davids, Gideons, Moseses, Hannahs, Esthers, Rahabs and even "Gomers" in the world, count it all joy. For God picked you out from all the others to be used by Him for His people and His purpose in the earth for Kingdom building.

Throughout my life I'd ask "why" on a regular basis.

I am a Child of God with no regrets. God has been with me through it ALL!!! Open your minds and "lend me your ears" and eyes-- to take you on a walk that had I'd known, what the answer would be...

In the forthcoming chain of events, some may consider them strange or even a fairytale; a dream or at times, a nightmare. But for me, this is my life. My name is Dr. Nathalie Chase Thompson.

CHAPTER 1

Look In The Mirror
Do "YOU" Like What "YOU" See?

Jeremiah 29:11 For I know my thoughts towards you says the LORD, thoughts of good not of evil to give you a future and a hope (NKJV)

Have you ever met a person that no matter what you say they've experienced it? Have you ever met a person that their life seems like a movie? Have you ever met that person that works your last nerve because they've been there and done that? Well, get ready, lock and load. (This is only eight years.) The number eight represents new beginnings.

Many Novembers

Today is November 18, 2014 it has been a bittersweet day. I began to search Google for my brother Leo C. Chase, JR.; (I was a little girl when he was taken from me.) I had found several listings reflecting on his service in Vietnam. On one of them I decided to enter a remembrance. Then looking at his profile I noticed the day of his death was November 15th. My father's Birthday is November 21. There are six days between the two; representing "a day of rest;" for on the 6th day Dominion was given unto every man that was made by God; and it was very good (suitable, pleasant) and HE approved it completely.

It wasn't until 2012 that I found out when it was my father's birthday. For forty-nine years of my life, I bore the name which held me in bondage. Although I always knew who my father was, it was always so hush-hush. My aunt would always tell me stories about him when they were growing up and how much I was like him.

Both of those men are resting in the bosom of Abraham. Although they are not here with me in the flesh, they are here in the spirit, so I rejoice. I never knew how important the month of November really was to me until now. At this time, I'm beginning the book, (53) years old and finally FREE.

Another type of Prison

All of us know of someone or we are that "someone" that was on the receiving end of dysfunction. You have that relative that's an alcoholic, on drugs, homosexual, lesbian, wannabe gangster or just plain stuck on stupid. But with all of these we can deal. The challenge is with the one that creates our prison.

You can be in a prison without being behind bars. This prison was one that was really very common, yet always kept quiet. This prison was commonly disguised as *"what goes on in the house stays in the house" rule.*

You may be thinking, "What prison?" It's called the "prison" of your mind. That prison where you create a fantasy world. That prison where you create make-believe people, family and friends. That prison where you are safe or at least you tell yourself you are. And if you are blessed to live through it, years later you ask yourself, "didn't anybody know? Didn't anybody see it? Didn't anybody hear? Why didn't anyone protect me?

Isaiah 54:17 **No weapon** that is formed against you will succeed; and every tongue which rise up against you in judgment you will condemn. This [peace, righteousness, security, and triumph over opposition] is the heritage of the servants of the Lord, and this is their vindication from Me, says the Lord. (AMP)

Wow, someone did see. Someone was there.

Can you believe this? Just from that small reflection I was now pushed into beginning this book. For years there had been prophecies spoken,

"You have to tell your story,"

"You have to get it out so others can live,"

I'm nervous, but my mind is going back in time like a movie being played out before me.

Who's delusional?

At this point one could become angry. Another option is looking into the mirror and asking yourself,

"What do YOU see?

This can be the beginning of a new day in your life all for the better or for the worse. The choice is yours.

Now for some people, they've gotten accustomed to this lifestyle or so they think it's become a natural part of their day-to-day life. The sad thing about this is that they have no sense of reality. They have no sense of as we say the "real world". If it's not chaotic if there is no drama, then they in fact think that there is a problem, and everyone else is strange. On the other hand, you have those that look at life and see everything with the pretty house the white picket fence 2.5 children. The husband and the wife-- a dog (and maybe a cat) and every day is "happy- happy joy- joy."

So, which one is more delusional?

Or the question should be, "why are they delusional?"

For every action there is a reaction for every cause there is an effect.

People in general, never take the time to ask the question why and what most people don't realize if the question is asked it could save so many lives. God has said, we are our brother's keeper. So why do you turn your back, give a deaf ear, shut your mouth and close your eyes? That is until it knocks on your door and then the earth must stand still and take notice. So again, who's delusional? Lord, have mercy.

Being true to yourself

Let's take the time to set the record straight. Because this book is going to touch so many different areas and so many different people's lives in so many different ways, be prepared.

Some may say I'm negative.

Some may say I'm still hurting.

Some may say I have no idea what I am talking about.

In addition, others may say I'm the delusional one.

Nevertheless, there is that small percentage that will **FULLY** understand and the prison gates **WILL FLY OPEN!!!!** And for you, may it be **THE FIRST DAY OF THE REST OF YOUR LIFE**. I really look forward to hearing from you! When this is all over, "said and done" all of us must look in the mirror and began to like what we see. The most important thing I've learned over the years is you have to be true to yourself.

Sometimes it will offend others. It will cause friendships to end. It can bring division among siblings. However, being true to you is not designed to destroy anyone. On the contrary, being true to oneself is designed to make you grow. With that being said, there is no way that I could have written this book without being true to me-- facing the good, bad and ugly; the indifference within me.

Psalms 139:23-24 Search me [thoroughly], O God, and know my heart! Try me and know my thoughts! And see if there is any wicked or hurtful way in me, and lead me in the way everlasting. (AMP)

JOURNAL your thoughts ~ BE FREE!!!!!!

Romans 8:18 For I consider [from the standpoint of faith] that the suffer-
ings of the present life are not worthy to be compared with the glory that
is about to be revealed to us and in us! (AMP)

_____

_____

_____

_____

_____

_____

_____

_____

_____

_____

_____

_____

_____

_____

_____

_____

And Now I Live

_____

_____

_____

_____

_____

_____

_____

_____

_____

_____

_____

_____

_____

_____

_____

_____

_____

_____

_____

_____

_____

_____

_____

_____

_____

_____

_____

CHAPTER 2

Thirteen going on Twenty:
Truth or Fantasy?

Ribault Middle School [1]

Junior High--this was a roller coaster ride. Now for some people, a roller coaster ride is exciting. For me it is not. Roller coasters remind me of my life as a child. They start out soft and slow and gradually raise the momentum, then, all of a sudden, a sudden stop. And then you drop, you turn.

There are screams!!!

There is fear.

There is excitement.

There is panic; there is joy.

You have no idea which way the experience is going to go. As quick as it starts, it stops.

The question is do you find yourself the same at the end of the ride as you were at the beginning?

All together that is?

I should have been having fun now in middle school sharing ties with friends finding out what subjects I liked and didn't like--having a good home life and family. NOT!!! I did not fit in at school. The girls didn't like me. I was always trying to make friends. The friends I was with were the wrong ones. Now don't get me wrong, there are those that to this day we have relationship. We have a friendship. We may not talk every day. We may not see each other all the time, but we have a love and great respect for one another. The best part is that some of us walk together in Ministry for Kingdom Building.

I was thirteen years old. I'd started smoking weed, drinking and had been having sex. No one at home knew, probably because I was invisible. I would stay gone a lot at that time. I didn't understand why I didn't like to go home, but I never wanted to be in the house by myself. I hung out with my older cousins who were more sisters and brothers than the ones in my house. Even with that, things were "hush-hush," (We're not even going to go into that area right now.)

Words can hurt you

I did very well in school, but the one area that I stood out the most in was chorus. Singing was an outlet. Singing was my happy place. It seemed to have always been. To this day singing and worship is in me.

Then I found myself on the volleyball team. The idea that I could take my frustrations out was like a real kick and a half for me seeing I already had to go through being talked about. When I had to put on those crazy looking gym outfits with the striped tops in the blue bottoms all one piece. I never showed my legs because I thought I was ugly and fat.

My sister use to tell me,

"You're not our sister."

"Nobody cares about you."

"Mama found you in a garbage dump."

"You were left at the hospital and mama felt sorry for your ugly behind and she brought you home."

21

I thought I was a charity case. It was easy to believe. I didn't look like either of my sisters, but I did look just like my two brothers. I was confused. It's crazy how words can shape your life. On top of that I had breast, small waist, big hips, butt and legs all at thirteen. I just thought I didn't fit in and when people said "you look good," it was hard to believe because of what I was getting from other places. I held true to what my sister said. These are supposed to be the people (family) that loved you the most, right? I thought everyone was lying and actually picking at me; now that was delusional.

Happy Times

So, like I said the girls didn't like me, but I had a lot of male friends. And yes, they were just friends. One reason the boys then they just acted silly so I was always attracted to older boys until this one person started hanging around me and we became best friends. We all were really good friends and what was the happiest time of my junior high time became a very dark place and started the spiral.

He and his sister went to visit their dad and they were coming back to Jacksonville across the bridge and a car loss control and hit their car and the car went off the bridge and they died. That messed me up because that was my "first love." My two brothers held me together. I was there shadow. Whenever they would go somewhere I was there the majority of the time. Unfortunately, one of them has transitioned and the other has lost memory of fifteen years. For him it is a coping method. I believe God will bring it back when he is ready. HE did it for me.

I would go with them and others, but there were those times when I would be left at home by myself. My God brothers Rickey and Gary would ride me on the motorcycles. We would hang out for hours. Those were happy times. Then at times my other brother, (which became more my brother-in-law,) would always take me when he and my sister would go out. I was at the drive-in with them. It had to aggravate her. Yes, I remember Milligan's--would get my hamburger, french fries and shake!

Those were brief "happy memories." Years later I realized this was his way of protecting me just as my older brother did. Thank God for Angels being encamped round about you, even when you are clueless. (LOL) Your Heavenly Father loves you.

A safe and peaceful place

Now the best part of these years was going to St. Augustine and over to my Aunt/Mama Bernice's house. "Big Red" was the REAL "Madea"[2] back there for us. Had the big Cadillac and was always packing. She had the three-story house with the wraparound porch. Every year the Queens would come through for their show and parade and would always stay at Big Red's house. She had a bedroom that converted into apartments. They would teach me and my cousin Arthurene how to dress and walk. It was crazy, but I loved it.

In St. Augustine I would be at the Funeral Home that my father founded, Leo C. Chase & Sons Funeral Home. But NO, I didn't stay there overnight. I stayed with my oldest brother and my sister-n-love. It was strange going sometimes, because whenever I got in trouble or needed something I was sent there. At times I would come home from school and this black car was waiting on me. *Funny I never needed clothes because Chase would go buy them when I got there, lol.*

When I was in trouble all he had to do was to look at me. I was done. I felt like I wanted to bury my head in a hole. Then he would have somebody take me and buy me something. I never took advantage of that. I loved that man and just to be with him was all I wanted; my safe and peaceful place.

There were other places like Hollywood, Fl for the summers with my Aunt Mary boy I did so much to this day my mama has no idea. Smell the cigar (Wilmington, NC) with my Uncle Melvin. Went fishing and going out on his boat--oh yeah and to camp for those two weeks. The only person I could be around smoking and it wouldn't trigger the wheezing or asthma. Right in town my Uncle Clarence and Aunt Ella, church, church and sitting at her feet listening to her tell me about my life and what God was going to do. Then she would line it up with the Word and pray me to sleep.

Tampa was with my Uncle Bubba and Aunt Margaret; they were older. That is where I got my first taste of Holiness Church, scrub boards, foot tubs, guitars you played laying in your lap. Mothers that would just make up songs and pray FOREVER!!!! I loved it! Those people stayed in church seven days a week and still raised children, worked, kept the house clean and tended to their husbands and wives. Both Aunt Ella and Aunt Margaret had rats the size of alley cats and spiders big as grapefruits. Jesus, I was scared to go to sleep. They would kill the rats but let the spiders live. Even typing that gives me the creeps.

All of them have transitioned. As long as I hew to the line I will see them again in Paradise.

*B*lessed assurance, Jesus is mine!
Oh, what a foretaste of glory divine!
Heir of salvation, purchase of God,
Born of His Spirit, washed in His blood.

This is my story, this is my song,
Praising my Savior all the day long;
This is my story, this is my song,
Praising my Savior all the day long.

Perfect submission, perfect delight,
Visions of rapture now burst on my sight;
Angels, descending, bring from above
Echoes of mercy, whispers of love.

Perfect submission, all is at rest,
I in my Savior am happy and blest,
Watching and waiting, looking above,
Filled with His goodness, lost in His love.

JOURNAL your thoughts ~ BE FREE!!!!!!

Psalm 143:7-8 Answer me quickly, LORD; my spirit fails(depression), Do not hide your face from me or I will be like those who go down to the pit. Let the morning bring me word of your unfailing love, for I have put my trust in you. Show me the way I should go, for to you I entrust my life.

_____

_____

_____

_____

_____

_____

_____

_____

_____

_____

_____

_____

_____

_____

_____

And Now I Live

_____

_____

_____

_____

_____

_____

_____

_____

_____

_____

_____

_____

_____

_____

_____

_____

_____

_____

_____

_____

_____

_____

_____

_____

_____

_____

_____

CHAPTER 3

My Hero's Syndrome

Remember when I said I couldn't really make friends and some of the friends I should have never made? Now this all stands from ages thirteen to fifteen, my junior high years. [Find yourself skipping school hanging out going and getting high smoking, drinking, having sex with older guys because you want to fit in.]

One of those days I didn't want to go and my friend insisted. We were going to go to my boyfriend's house because I need to get something and then over to my house. This was a classic set up and I was clueless.

We get to the boyfriend's house and while we're there, she and the boyfriend go in and have sex. I'm sitting in the living room looking at the TV and the next thing you know, a couple other guys come in. I'm drinking a soda and I have to walk away. I come back, I finished my drink and then I'm not feeling well.

"Oh well, you know,"

"Let us take you home and you'll be alright."

[My friend comes out.]

"I'll go with you, nobody is there right,"

"You'll be able to go in and go to sleep before your sister gets home from school."

I'm out of it. I can't keep my eyes open. I'm extremely drowsy and very nauseous and I vaguely remember getting in the front seat. She's sitting next to me and the boyfriend is driving so there are three of us in the front. However, the guys that came over jump in the car. They were just going to ride with him to take me home. I had no idea there was a second car that followed. She and the boyfriend helped me to the door. She came in with me to make sure everything was straight.

"You go ahead and lay down"

"I'll lock the door when I leave"

The next thing I know, someone is on top of me. Before he gets up, there was another one, and again and again. In fact, there were seven of them. That was called back then a "Georgia train" today it's known as "gang rape."

I thought I was hollering. I felt like I was fighting.

No matter what I did they wouldn't stop.

They actually started a second round.

One of the guys realized that I was crying and was fighting them. I was screaming and he stopped them and he made them leave.

This was now "My hero." This is called the Hero Syndrome. He put me in the shower and I remember shaking so bad because it was a cold shower and I wanted to get out.

[He kept telling me]

"No, stand under the water.

 I need to wake you up."

Then he fixed something hot. I cannot recall if it was coffee or tea. He sat with me until I came around. He apologized because he thought "I wanted it." Mainly because everyone else she would bring was game. They knew what to expect. He made sure I was alright and alert. Then he leaves.

I wouldn't dare telling anybody, (thinking to myself) because nobody would ever believe it. I didn't even believe it. It didn't happen once, it happened twice. If you are delusional, you will think that there is no way you are going to get caught up in the same situation again. If you skip school, get high, are drinking and hanging out with your so-called friends trust me, it will happen again or worse.

It happened again.

The reason why in my opinion: guilt by association.

While walking home with a true friend through the Washington Heights path, they jumped out of the bushes and grabbed me. I wished they would have just killed me and gotten it over with. All of a sudden one of them started screaming and yelled for the others to go. They were being hit and couldn't see where it was coming from. I didn't know then, but I know now they were my warring Angels fighting for me. And this lady and man came and got me up and took care of me. It was as if I was dreaming. I can't tell you how I made it to the girl's house after all of that.

JOURNAL your thoughts ~ BE FREE!!!!!!

I Corinthians 13:1-3 If I speak in the tongues[a] of men or of angels, but do not have love, I am only a resounding gong or a clanging cymbal. If I have the gift of prophecy and can fathom all mysteries and all knowledge, and if I have a faith that can move mountains, but do not have love, I am nothing. If I give all I possess to the poor and give over my body to hardship that I may boast, but do not have love, I gain nothing (NIV)

_____

_____

_____

_____

_____

_____

_____

_____

_____

_____

_____

_____

_____

_____

_____

_____

And Now I Live

And Now I Live

CHAPTER 4

The Sprint

Oh boy! I've graduated from dealing with young boys and senior high boys. I'm fifteen and I find myself "dating" a twenty-nine year old. This situation sounds crazy within itself right? It gets better. He's taking me back and forth to school. He's getting my school supplies. He is helping me with my school work. I'm staying with him sometimes weeks at a time--the whole nine yards.

Some of you may be saying, "Where is your mom, your sisters and your brothers?" They all were in their own (mental) place. They were wherever they needed to be at the time. They weren't there, if that makes sense. People can be around you and you can still be by yourself. You can be in a house full of people and still be by yourself.

My mother knew about it. In fact she knew his mom and other relatives. When he would come over, they would talk. They got along wonderfully. I didn't understand it until much later what was happening. All was fine with her until I got pregnant. Again I'm fifteen and he is twenty-nine years old. First of all, if the law had found out he and my mom could have been arrested for statutory rape and child neglect.

With what logic?

One could say,

"How can that be statutory rape when your mother was in agreement with it?"

It wasn't like she was not aware that I was having sex. Who can really answer what was logical behind that.

I just knew what I was doing, and now I was pregnant.

I get sent to Tampa quietly because I was "jeopardizing her reputation" and I had to have an abortion. I remember that vividly because they kept telling me to stop fighting. I was fighting the suction when they stuck the tube inside of me. I begin to feel the pull when they had examined me. They said I was over two months. Basically the baby was being pulled apart inside of me. The abortion was very difficult on my body. It was extremely difficult on my mind. This was the first time I felt like my sister cared. She handled me so carefully and watched over me. WOW I had a sister.

When I came back to Jacksonville I told him, and he went off on my mom. It didn't stop us from seeing each other. At that point he wanted me to move in with him. Then it was absolutely "NOT." I don't understand the logic of that to this day.

Me on the run

Since she wouldn't let me, I ran away from home. I ended up at a house on Moncrief. I met a young lady who just befriended me. (She actually lived on the corner of 26th Street and Chase.) I remember there was a red light on the porch at night, but we were on Moncrief just past the cleaners. There were always men going in and out of the house. I didn't think anything of it. They were having orgies, sharing drugs, needles and everything else. Guess what? I never participated. I was like Hazel cooking and cleaning why they did whatever they were doing. There were times that a couple of the guys wanted to approach me. There was a guy that was there by the name of Michael that wouldn't allow them to. He was my protector (hero syndrome).

Because of times past and what I've heard, and what I

had seen, "you have to reward" those that are there for you to protect you. The only thing I learned was to have sex with them. He wouldn't touch me. He never would. I thought that was so crazy, but he wouldn't. One night I knew he had been drinking and smoking so I approached him. When he woke up, I was already on top of him. He stopped because he said it was wrong.

By that time my cousin knew where I was and had my mom send the police to get me. I was ticked off with her. I knew who and what were waiting at the house for me. When I got there, mama told me to go take a shower and clean up. Well I did and when I got out of the shower she came in the room with this WIDE LEATHER belt. Lord Jesus, this woman had NEVER whipped me before Thank you Jesus!!!! But she wore my behind out. Then went to work and I left right behind her. I WAS NOT STAYING IN THAT HOUSE!!! Trust me it will all become clear in Volume 2 of the And Now I Live series "The Silence is Broken". (Time lines need to be thrown out of your mind on this journey.)

(Psalms 35:1-3) "PLEAD my cause, O LORD, with those who strive with me; Fight against those who fight against me. Take hold of shield and buckler, And stand up for my help. Also draw out the spear, And stop those who pursue me. Say to my soul, 'I am your salvation.''

Great is Thy faithfulness, O God my Father
There is no shadow of turning with Thee
Thou changest not, Thy compassions, they fail not
As Thou hast been, Thou forever will be

Summer and winter and springtime and harvest
Sun, moon and stars in their courses above
Join with all nature in manifold witness
To Thy great faithfulness, mercy and love

Great is Thy faithfulness
Great is Thy faithfulness
Morning by morning new mercies I see
All I have needed Thy hand hath provided
Great is Thy faithfulness, Lord, unto me

Pardon for sin and a peace that endureth
Thine own dear presence to cheer and to guide
Strength for today and bright hope for tomorrow
Blessings all mine, with ten thousand beside

Great is Thy faithfulness (great is Thy faithfulness)
Great is Thy faithfulness
Morning by morning new mercies I see
All I have needed Thy hand hath provided
Great is Thy faithfulness, Lord, unto me

And Now I Live

JOURNAL your thoughts ~ BE FREE!!!!!!

Genesis 50:17a This is what you are to say to Joseph: I ask you to forgive your brothers the sin and the wrongs they committed in treating you so badly. (NIV)

_____

_____

_____

_____

_____

_____

_____

_____

_____

_____

_____

_____

_____

_____

_____

_____

_____

CHAPTER 5

The Set Back

Ok, the police have brought me home to an empty house. Tick tock tick tock LOUD in my ears, sounding like a real clock, it was my heart beat. WOW! Now I'm home in the shower y'all. My mom whipped me and my stepfather was standing there. I was butt wet naked in front of both of them. I remember the look in his eyes as though this is pleasing to him. Not so much of me getting a whipping, but the sight of me was pleasing to him.

49

Then I remembered when he would come to the house drunk. If I was in the shower he will come in the bathroom and pull the shower curtain to just stand there. Or in the room getting dressed, he would bust in the door and would just stand there when I was half naked. He did not bother me because I was very vocal. I would have said something and would prob-ably have hurt him after the first episode.

> "at the time I still didn't know the red light meant it was a whorehouse."

Red lights and things

A couple months later, in fact ended up on 26th and Chase Street again with that red light outside the house-- at the time I still didn't know the red light meant it was a whorehouse. So I ended up with Donna again. She was taking care of me getting you know, to get close. I've taken all types of pills. Purple and chocolate microdots, window pain, snorted much cocaine and smoked plenty of weed. (Never did care much for drinking though.)

I ended up out 21st just before Buckman St, to this pool hall that had rooms built onto the back like a little motel. Donna was getting me ready to start turning tricks. I've had a "Mickey" slipped to me, and I drank some Cognac. This big, ugly, fat man comes in smelling of liquor. He starts to grope and kiss all over me. I was about to kick him to sleep.

He proceeds to tell me,

"You know what you're here for.

Why are you fighting?

I just paid for you."

    I gave him some words on how much I didn't give a blankety-blank blank what he paid; he was not going to touch me. He finally asked me how old I was. Even though I told him that I was sixteen, he said I that didn't look it and he paid his money. I was cussing him out because I didn't care. I can laugh now. But do you realize he could've killed me? Oh my goodness. Finally he stopped trying and began telling me what I was getting myself into. He said I needed to get away from them because it was going to get worse. I could run across somebody that wasn't going to let up as easy. The police come once again and took me home.

And Now I Live

JOURNAL your thoughts ~ BE FREE!!!!!!

Philippians 1:6 I am convinced and confident of this very thing, that He who has begun a good work in you will [continue to] perfect and complete it until the day of Christ Jesus [the time of His return]. (AMP)

_____

_____

_____

_____

_____

_____

_____

_____

_____

_____

_____

_____

_____

_____

_____

_____

_____

_____
_____
_____
_____
_____
_____
_____
_____
_____
_____
_____
_____
_____
_____
_____
_____
_____
_____
_____
_____
_____
_____
_____
_____

CHAPTER 6

The Set Up

This time coming home was different because I was getting ready to get the shock of my life. My brother was stationed in Japan. Unbeknown to me my mother had told him about the first incident, my behavior, and me running away. While I was gone, she apparently reached out to him and he was able to come home. Well, my mom was working 3-11. She called home and told me to hurry up and get out of the house.

I'm not understanding, why she told me to hurry up and leave. We have a tendency of doing things out of emotions and not thinking about all the consequences of our actions. Well I didn't get out. I didn't leave.

I went to open the door and my brother walked in. He was in his military fatigues with his steel toed boots and before I knew it, he hit me. He started kicking me. I have a bruise to this day from him kicking me with those boots on. I remember him saying that he would kill me before allowing me to kill my mom from worrying her. (Again, someone acting out of their emotions and rage.) He finally came to himself and stopped. He was the one that I was always his shadow before he left for the service. He just left the house without a word. Today he has no memory of at least fifteen years of his life. People have different ways of suppressing tragic events. And although we have a crazy relationship now, that's still my brother and I love him. How many mess ups have you created and didn't know how to back paddle out of them?

Neighborhood entertainment

I was still at the house. My stepfather comes home. He's drunk as Kooter Brown. He's so drunk until he did one of his outside performances. He pulls up on the grass. He gets out of the car stands up in the yard and begins to urinate in the middle of the yard. There were people walking up and down the street and he doesn't care. He then gets up on the car, lies up on top of the hood and just begins to masturbate on the car. He holds himself and goes to sleep. I'm asking him to come in the house and I get cussed out. It wasn't embarrassing anymore because everybody was accustomed to it. To a couple of people on our street this was like their entertainment for the week.

Once again you may ask where everyone else was. My oldest sister graduated from high school, she left and went to college, my other sister was there, but she was never home and my mom was working.

Are you kidding me?

So now I've become immune to all of it. I had to sleep in his room and at times in bed with him if he came home from work. My mom had her room and my sister had hers. LORD I HATE THIS!!! Did anybody see something wrong with this picture? So I was glad when my sister left. I finally got a room to myself at sixteen. Everyone is gone, I can breathe. At least I thought.

He was staying down at Ponte Vedra Bch where he worked. Don't have to deal with that foolishness anymore, WRONG! It actually had gone up a notch or two. He knew I would fight him now, funny but true. So he resorts to threats with his gun. OMG he was known for pulling it on you in a heartbeat. Then the day after not recalling anything, that was found to be a lie. Those who drink on a regular at some point become numb to the side effects, i.e. lost of memory. For if you listen to conversations with friends they laugh about the incidents. Several of us have compared notes over the years.

I need Thee, oh I need Thee
Every hour I need Thee
Oh bless me now my Savior
I come to Thee

I need Thee every hour
Most gracious Lord
No tender voice like Thine
Can peace afford

I need Thee every hour
Stay close and nearby
Temptations be their power
When You are close by

I need Thee, oh I need Thee
Every hour I need Thee
Oh bless me now my Savior
I come to Thee

And Now I Live

JOURNAL your thoughts ~ BE FREE!!!!!!

Joshua 1:7 Only be thou strong and very courageous, that thou mayest ob-
serve to do according to all the law, which Moses my servant commanded
thee: turn not from it to the right hand or to the left, that thou mayest
prosper withersoever thou goest.

_____

_____

_____

_____

_____

_____

_____

_____

_____

_____

_____

_____

_____

_____

_____

_____

_____

And Now I Live

_____

_____

_____

_____

_____

_____

_____

_____

_____

_____

_____

_____

_____

_____

_____

_____

_____

_____

_____

_____

_____

_____

_____

CHAPTER 7

Your Perception Your Reality

Yes, I've been raped twice by now and attempted suicide with class 3 narcotics. Believe me I didn't take any of this lightly. Although I look like I'm in my early twenties, I was still sixteen. Was working out every day, had my first job working in the warehouse of Busch Beer and Toyota car boat yard. I was making very good money.

Yet even with that I was being passed around by family members to friends like a piece of meat. Slipping into night clubs and the owners knew me personally and let me in. While they knew what was happening.

Classic lie

I didn't look at any of these things as being abusive or destructive because they said "they loved me" and wanted to be with me. Classic lie, but you know ---I'd gotten so accustomed to it. It was a natural part of life for me by then. Being beat on had become a form of caring and loving and the topper then we jumped into bed. If you didn't, you didn't care about me. How many of you have found yourself in some of these same places feeling and thinking some of the very same things. Yet through it all, I'm passing my classes with good grades, going to church and singing in the choir. I faithfully would read Faith Books and the Bible, why because GOD had HIS hand upon me ALL the while. I thought I was crazy most of the time. I had created this life inside my life. Unbeknown to me it was my ministering angels comforting me through my journey.

Isaiah 26:2-4 (NIV)

Open the gates that the righteous nation may enter, the nation that keeps faith, You will keep in perfect peace those whose minds are steadfast, because they trust in you. Trust in the LORD forever, for the LORD himself, is the Rock eternal.

JOURNAL your thoughts ~ BE FREE!!!!!!

Philippians 12:1-2a Wherefore seeing we also are compassed about with so great a cloud of witnesses, let us lay aside every weight, and the sin which doth so easily beset us, and let us run with patience the race that is set before us. Looking unto Jesus the author and finisher of our faith

_____

_____

_____

_____

_____

_____

_____

_____

_____

_____

_____

_____

_____

_____

CHAPTER 8

Denial 101

Here I was at the club in my boyfriend's car with the girls. This fine looking man pulls up next to us. He speaks and the earth stood still it seemed. In one night he became my "god". Mind you I did say I was in my "boyfriend's" car, the mess up of the century doing that to him. For the next seven years, this man was my world. He wined and dined me, showered me with gifts and we were like rabbits. Well at seventeen, I found myself pregnant, by another twenty-nine year old man. I didn't know it because I wasn't showing and my menstrual cycle was still coming for six months.

Just read the letter

Everything was going fine. He moves me out from my mom's house. Then eventually ole boy moves me into the motel/studios on Main Street. One day he's home I'm in class at FJC. He finds a letter I've written to my ex and all hell broke out. He tries to kill me --goodness I have an iron pipe across my throat chocking me. The sad part about it, he never asked why the letter was written.

Well I was writing to tell my ex, I'd found someone that I felt was turning my life around for the better. Someone that I felt really loved me, (what a joke.) Thanking him for every-thing that he had done etc. Now someone trying to kill me because they think that I'm betraying them? All he had to do was to read the letter.

Five miles home

After that incident, again I tried to kill both me and my unborn son. They had to rush me to the hospital because of the pills I'd taken. Then back home with him I go. Hey, my mom has no idea. A few days later we're downtown to the fountain at the bridge and he's apologizing, he wants to go for the weekend for change of scenery but I don't want to stay. OMG I didn't respond like he wanted, and he begins to hoop and holler at me in the car. He slaps me so the beating began. I'm seven months now I get my crazy self out of the car and began to walk across Main Street Bridge. Mind you my mom lived off Ave B & 45th Street, which was more than five miles. And yes, I walked the entire way to the house. Wearing a pair of black shorts, sandals with a yellow and black top, I was so swollen by the time I got home. I was miserable and sick as a dog. At least I'm safe or so I thought I was until my stepfather showed up.

I got it "wrong" again

I was getting ready to be put out because I was pregnant. God stepped in. I was able to get an apartment down the street in Alameda St., Apartments-- apartment 122. Before the apartment was ready I was staying with who I thought was my best friend. I had my son twenty-four hours and twenty-six minutes of long and hard labor, and delivery. The temperature was in the 100's while I was in the hospital.

Nine months later I found myself pregnant again. When I met "my man" I had no idea he was married and separated from his wife who was missing in action. (He actually moved me into his house. When then she decided to come home because she found out about me. So that's how we ended up on Main Street.)

What a joke!

Throughout our seven year relationship I went through a

busted eardrum, busted ribs, black eyes, spat on, stabbed with ice picks and all sorts of lovely things with this one man. Yet I was refusing to leave because I didn't want a failed relationship; what a joke. All through this I was working and in college. I knew how to cover up the bruises and put on my happy face.

We never truly think of the children through the abuse, although we say we do. What we're really doing is trying to save face. Especially if you were already told you'd never be anything; nobody wants you, or this one, "you only good for a quick lay." How many of you have found yourself on that end? Or better yet, you were the giver. You actually dished out the abuse and you were their abuser. It doesn't matter. At the beginning of the book I spoke about being in a prison. This was one of them.

Nobody but You, Lord,
Nobody but You.
Nobody but You, Lord,
Nobody but You.
When I was in trouble,
You came to my rescue;
Nobody but You, Lord,
Nobody but You.

Lord, You healed the sick
And You raised the dead.
With two fishes and five loaves of bread,
Five thousand souls You fed.
If You did it back then,
You can do it again; nobody but You, Lord,
Nobody but You.

And Now I Live

JOURNAL your thoughts ~ BE FREE!!!!!!

Isaiah 41:10 Fear thou not; for I am with thee: be not dismayed; for I am thy
God: I will strengthen thee; yea, I will help thee; yea, I will uphold thee with
the right hand of my righteousness

_____

_____

_____

_____

_____

_____

_____

_____

_____

_____

_____

_____

_____

_____

_____

And Now I Live

CHAPTER 9

Shock & Awe

I remember one Saturday morning my mom finding out a lot because I had a black eye. She was taking me to work at Florida Times Union.

She said,

"Is he just that important to you that you're willing to let him kill you?

One thing you should always remember, nobody can raise your children like you can, if you are alive to raise them".

My Mama has a way with words. What she didn't know was that I was beaten all night long based on a lie that was told. The sad part, my children were brought into the room to watch him. And after the beating, he got sick and I cleaned him up. This is not strange for so many people both men and women alike. This was becoming a bi-weekly chain of events. Yet daily, I went to work for The United States Marine Corp Recruiting Station & Florida Times Union lol. I have to think about that now, Lord how sick I was. You think someone was praying for me. Throughout all of this so far I'm only twenty-years old.

My kids are off limits

Now his beating on me didn't make me leave him. In fact, he beat me so bad at one point because he'd been drinking 150 Proof Vodka and his "friend" told him he had slept with me, He came in and commits to wearing me out so much to the point he grabbed both of our kids in one arm and threw me across the room. He had them sitting on the sofa watching. That didn't even stop me from being with him. What did however-- was a day at a Catholic school carnival. My son saw him and ran to him. He was with the wife and son.

My son came back crying because he was told,

"Get out of my face and go back with your mom."

Do what you will to me, but, you will not hurt my children! I went home made a call for my locks to be changed and I set all of his things outside the door. So when he came home (because he was living with me, not with the wife) his things were packed up. This had begun the first of many changes that would later bring me to where I am today. For as my spiritual father would say, 'Judge your future by your past." I am a female Job "Picked Out To Be Picked On"--Bishop A.T. Jones, Sr. As well as a female Joseph, yet it is well with my soul. Funny, because I hadn't met Bishop Jones yet guess I was getting prepared. Only you have the power to come out of your prison. The Lord has given us freedom of choice.

> "Only you have the power to come out of your prison. The Lord has given us freedom of choice."

This book is a "small" part of what life has handed me. BUT I'M STILL HERE!!!! Well some would say I haven't read anything positive. I disagree. The positive is this; I'm here to write about it. Most people look at the glass have empty, I look and see it half full on its way to running over. Every situation and/or circumstance is a life lesson. We walk always learning the good, bad, and indifferent.

In the end it's what we do with these lessons that will make or break us. Remember that prison is not always behind barbed wire and steel gates. The worst prison is locked away in your inner self. We must never allow an "inner me" to become an "enemy." Take your power back!

For all the "black sheep, misfits and cast-a-ways" YOU ARE COUNTED AMONGST THE GREAT!!!

JOURNAL your thoughts ~ BE FREE!!!!!!

Romans 8:28 and we know that all things work together for good to them that love God, to them who are the called according to his purpose.

_____

_____

_____

_____

_____

_____

_____

_____

_____

_____

_____

_____

_____

_____

_____

_____

_____

And Now I Live

_____

_____

_____

_____

_____

_____

_____

_____

_____

_____

_____

_____

_____

_____

_____

_____

_____

_____

_____

_____

_____

_____

CHAPTER 10

My Conclusion Is This:

Do you realize just how important it is to have clear communication? When you know there is someone you can talk to it can make a world of difference in your life. Even realizing that we do act out through our emotions, we still come to a reality that before we carry out our actions, we should talk! I know for a fact most reading if you have younger siblings you've taken a few whippings and punishments because of the younger sibling. Some of those were simply because no questions were asked or you weren't able to plead your case. Through communication you will even find out that you're not alone even within your own family or circles.

Listen to the silence screams from our children; those born of us and those around us. Every person both young and old that acts out is not always because they are being defiant. Some truly have had NO training, yet they've trained themselves the art of survival of the fittest. Don't be so busy that you become deaf and blind to what is happening around you. For others, to what is happening IN you.

In so many cases we lie to ourselves to fit in, to please others, to mask our pain and much more. As in the story of Snow White the Queen had the looking glass mirror that lied to her. Well at some point in our life we have to pull the bandage off and clean that sore out. Regardless that it hurts. Walk through the looking glass; you may see your true self. I've learned how to see me, NOT who others say I am. I challenge you to be true to yourself as you walk out your own process. Nobody can walk your process out but you. Quit depending on friends to do what only you can do for you.

As you go through life we choose our "friends" not always for the right reasons, some are just a way of escape, later to find out it was a trap. We want friends or others to come in a rescue us and to be some type of hero. For we were all taught that a "hero" is always the good guy; your mom, dad, coach or someone you admire from a distance. Well is some peoples life their hero's don't always start out being the "good guy" truth be told they never will truly be the "good guy" but our minds convince us they are. You say, "That can't be." You will soon discover if you haven't already, that the mind truly is a terrible thing to waste.

I encourage you to grow and continue in your journey. You will experience those times you want "this" to hurry up and be over. Well whatever your "this" is may be in the will of God. Everything we go through may not always come from God but HE will work through it if we give it to Him. Even when we don't walk with Him as we should be it young or old HE is always present with us. Our rippled effects may catch someone at their breaking point and be a saving grace. So you see our mess ups can be a set up!

The words written in this book were not from a dark place. In reality they are from a very wealthy place. The book was not written to expose others but to FREE the person within. We create walls and make-believe worlds--but at some point we must live in the real world! Forgiveness, healing and peace are things we can obtain. However, we must be aware of the voices we allow in our ears. My hope is that you will be the voice for others that are caught still within their fantasy world of the mind. Dare to be a mouth-piece for someone that has no voice. I promise it will change your life! It was truly by the Grace of God, HE loved me when I couldn't see, hear or feel. Thank God for being a misfit in man's eyes and being a princess in God's eyes; and now I live.

A change, a change has come over me.
He changed my life and now I'm free.
He washed away all my sins, and He made me whole,
He washed me white as snow.

He changed, my life complete, and now I sit
I sit at His feet. To do what must be done
I'll work and work, until He comes
A wonderful change has come over me
A wonderful change has come over me

Changed
I'm so glad You changed me

And Now I Live

JOURNAL your thoughts ~ BE FREE!!!!!!

Romans 8:38-39 For I am persuaded, that neither death, nor life, nor angels, nor principalities, nor powers, nor things present, nor things to come,Nor height, nor depth, nor any other creature, shall be able to separate us from the love of God, which is in Christ Jesus our Lord.

CHAPTER 11

Stay Focused For Real

There are twelve Bible verses that keep me on point and focused. If you embrace them and live them, they too will not only encourage you, but will help you obtain and keep the great things about to come your way.

Jeremiah 29:10-11 For thus saith the LORD, That after seventy years be accomplished at Babylon I will visit you, and perform my good word toward you, in causing you to return to this place. For I know the thoughts that I think toward you, saith the LORD, thoughts of peace, and not of evil, to give you an expected end.

God never just allows things to happen. There's always a purpose an plan.

Mark 14:36 And he said, Abba, Father, all things are possible unto thee; take away this cup from me: nevertheless not what I will, but what thou wilt.

We face challenges just like Jesus but as Jesus did we must come to the place it's not about us nor what we want but the will of the Father.

Job 14:1 Man that is born of a woman is of few days and full of trouble.

As long as you live you will be faced with problems. Just keep on living.

Zephaniah 1:7 Hold thy peace at the presence of the Lord GOD: for the day of the LORD is at hand: for the LORD hath prepared a sacrifice, he hath bid his guests.

The Lord has specifically called for me and prepared GREATNESS for me on HIS behalf.

Psalm 66:18-19 If I regard iniquity in my heart, the Lord will not hear me: But verily God hath heard me; he hath attended to the voice of my prayer.

Holding onto anger and unforgiveness is like a cancer that

will spread and kill everything that is good. Forgive and move forward. Forgiveness is not for the other person, but for you.

2 Corinthians 13:5 Examine yourselves, whether ye be in the faith; prove your own selves. Know ye not your own selves, how that Jesus Christ is in you, except ye be reprobates?

Be true to you.

Judges 16:21-22 But the Philistines took him, and put out his eyes, and brought him down to Gaza, and bound him with fetters of brass; and he did grind in the prison house. Howbeit the hair of his head began to grow again after he was shaven.

Even in your darkest times if you allow the Lord to be God and The Holy Ghost to lead, you will overcome any obstacle placed before you. Get out of your feelings.

Mark 11:25 And when ye stand praying, forgive, if ye have ought against any: that your Father also which is in heaven may forgive you your trespasses.

If you want God to act on your behalf, make sure you are in right standing first. Get it straight so it (your request) will last and not just visit you.

Ephesians 4:32 And be ye kind one to another, tenderhearted, forgiving one another, even as God for Christ's sake hath forgiven you.

Show kindness, forgiveness and love to others daily, and watch how much sweeter your life will be.

1 Thessalonians 5:12 And we beseech you, brethren, to know them which labour among you, and are over you in the Lord, and admonish you;

Be mindful of the people within your inner circle. Are they a asset or liability to and for you? There is nothing wrong with starting the circle over again-- that's called wisdom.

Isaiah 41:9 Thou whom I have taken from the ends of the earth, and called thee from the chief men thereof, and said unto thee, Thou art my servant; I have chosen thee, and not cast thee away.

It's good to know that God didn't cast me away but purposely pulled me up and out for His glory.

Habakkuk 2:1-4 I will stand upon my watch, and set me upon the tower, and will watch to see what he will say unto me, and what I shall answer when I am reproved. And the LORD answered me, and said, Write the vision, and make it plain upon tables, that he may run that readeth it. For the vision is yet for an appointed time, but at the end it shall speak, and not lie: though it tarry, wait for it; because it will surely come, it will not tarry. Behold, his soul which is lifted up is not upright in him: but the just shall live by his faith.

Watch as well as pray. Be willing to do what is told you, even in the face of those that fight against you. Stay focused, dream, launch out and believe. You can do that when you have a relationship with God

JOURNAL your thoughts ~ BE FREE!!!!!!

I Corinthians 5:17 Therefore if any man be in Christ, he is a new creature: old things are passed away; behold, all things are become new.

_____

_____

_____

_____

_____

_____

_____

_____

_____

_____

_____

_____

_____

_____

_____

_____

And Now I Live

CHAPTER 12

DECLARATION

Dedicated Service Romans 12:1-2

Therefore I urge you, brothers and sisters, by the mercies of God, to present your bodies [dedicating all of yourselves, set apart] as a living sacrifice, holy and well-pleasing to God, which is your rational (logical, intelligent) act of worship.

And do not be conformed to this world [any longer with its superficial values and customs], but be transformed and progressively changed [as you mature spiritually] by the renewing of your mind [focusing on godly values and ethical attitudes], so that you may prove [for yourselves] what the will of God is, that which is good and acceptable and perfect [in His plan and purpose for you]. (AMP)

If you agree to this make an outward show and commit-ment by signing the Dedicated Service Agreement. This is for you as a vow made to God regarding Romans 12:1-2.

_____

Date _____

Thank you! You are in my thoughts and prayers.

Look for Volume 2 of And Now I Live, "The Silence Is Broken"

Will your heart and soul say yes?
Will your Spirit still say yes?
There is more that I require of thee
Will your heart and soul say yes?

Now will your heart and soul say yes?
Will your Spirit still say yes?
If I told you what I really need
Will your heart and soul say yes?

My soul says YES

ABOUT THE AUTHOR

Dr. Nathalie Chase Thompson, Founder of LifesReDesign Ministry International, Inc. & President of Habakkuk 2 School of Ministry, has served in ministry for almost 32 years in numerous capacities-- from administration & leadership, teaching and evangelism, to prophetic ministry and exhortation. Regardless of the task, she has been faithful to the cause of Christ. Dr. Thompson has provided outreach services and personal coaching to families, the sick and those incarcerated. As a believer in empowerment and education of all people, she has developed a variety of programs, workshops, seminars which give back to others what God, (by His grace) has given to her, a life "Re-Design".

Dr. Thompson is a graduate of both Jones Business College and St. Thomas Christian University, and was recently affirmed as an (Apostle) by Apostle Dave Ragan of Harvest Ministries Jacksonville Florida. She has five children and six grandchildren all currently living in Florida, and has become "mama" to both young and old over the years.

DR. NATHALIE CHASE THOMPSON

LifesReDesign Ministry International, Inc.
http://www.LifesReDesignMinistry.org ~ (904) 419-9224

Habakkuk 2 School of Ministry (Affiliate of Isaiah University)
http://www.habakkuk2som.org ~ (904) 701-8813

Ex-Offenders Operation Faith Transition Transportation and
Re-Development Program http://www.opfaith.org ~ (904)
289-1961

And Now I Live

She's faced the hardest times you could imagine
And many times her eyes fought back the tears
And when her youthful world was about to fall in
Each time her slender shoulders bore the weight of all her fears
And a sorrow no one hears
Still rings in midnight silence in her ears

Let her cry, for she's a lady (She's a lady)
Let her dream, for she's a child (Child)
Let the rain fall down upon her
She's a free and gentle flower growing wild

And if by chance that I should hold her (If by chance that I should hold
her) Let me hold her for a time (Let me hold her for a time)
And if allowed just one possession
I would pick her from the garden to be mine (I would pick her from the
garden to be mine)

Be careful how you touch her, for she'll awaken
And sleep's the only freedom that she knows
And when you walk into her eyes, you won't believe
The way she's always payin' for a debt she never owed
And a silent wind still blows
That only she can hear, and so she goes

Let her cry, for she's a lady
Let her dream, for she's a child
Let the rain fall down upon her
She's a free and gentle flower growing wild

Let her cry, for she's a lady (She's a lady)
Let her dream, for she's a child
Let the rain fall down upon her
She's a free and gentle flower growing wild
She's a flower growing wild
She's free

114

ACKNOWLEDGEMENTS continued...

Apostles Timothy & Pamela Williams whom I've known for years. They've covered me, encouraged me and walked through my early years in Ministry with me. Their words of encouragement and just watching their life has given me a drive to press on ahead.

Chief Apostle LaShawn M. & General Overseer Muneerah Crawford, Jr. these two young people in age but Old in The Spirit. I thank God for the timing of God, and having a listening ear. They PUSH HARD but with a lot of love. Even more they pull you as well when you're weak and weary.

Apostle Eddie Maxie & Pastor Karen Givner, Jr. I had the honor to meet them at my Affirmation Svc in 2015 in Orlando, FL. They both had to evaluate me and believe me they did and still are guiding me in the ways of God. It's from Genesis to Revelations no wavering and if so GET UP and get back on it. I love you both.

Apostle Roy & Prophetess EShawnna Smith they both embraced me IN TRUTH. Meeting Apostle Roy Etienne Smith was a divine appointment of God. He knows me and for that I'm grateful.

To Apostle Dave & Jennifer Ragan: This statement will forever be with me, "You've been in bondage for so long, you don't ever realize when you are FREE" Thank you!

To everyone else that I didn't mention. So many played a part in the process and are yet still here, good, bad or indifferent. Blessing of god be unto you all. I love you

ENDNOTES

1   Jean Ribault Middle School, Duval County Public School System--Jacksonville, FL

2   Madea is a fictional character created by Producer, Actor and Film Director, Tyler Perry.

3   Blessed Assurance Lyrics-- Francis J. Crosby [public domain]

4   Great is Thy Faithfulness Lyrics ©1923. Hope Publishing

5   Nobody but You Lord Lyrics-- Mahailia Jackson, BMG Management

6   Changed Lyrics-- Walter Hawkins, Capitol Christian Music Group

7   I Need Thee Every Hour Lyrics-- [public domain]

8   "Yes" Lyrics ©Spirit Music Group

9   Wildflower Lyrics ©1972. Dave Richardson & Doug Edwards

JOURNAL your thoughts ~ BE FREE!!!!!!

Psalms 37:23-24 The steps of a good man are ordered by the Lord: and he delighteth in his way. Though he fall, he shall not be utterly cast down: for the Lord upholdeth him with his hand.

_____

_____

_____

_____

_____

_____

_____

_____

_____

_____

_____

_____

_____

_____

_____

_____

_____